GASHMU SAITH IT

GASHMU SAITH IT

How to Build Christian Communities that Save the World

DOUGLAS WILSON

canonpress
Moscow, Idaho

Published by Canon Press
P.O. Box 8729, Moscow, Idaho 83843
800.488.2034 | www.canonpress.com
Printed in the United States of America.

Douglas Wilson, *Gashmu Saith It: How to Build Christian Communities that Save the World*
Copyright ©2021 by Douglas Wilson.

Cover design by James Engerbretson.
Interior layout by Valerie Anne Bost.

Endsheets: LCHS Photograph Collection 01-01-084. This historical map of Moscow, Idaho is used by permission and with thanks to the Latah County Historical Society.

Library of Congress Cataloging-in-Publication Data forthcoming:

21 22 23 21 22 23 24 25   10 9 8 7 6 5 4 3 2 1

*This book is dedicated
to the memory of Gashmu.*

CONTENTS

INTRODUCTION

The point of this small book will be to help the reader to better understand the crisis of our times, along with the demeanor we as Christians are called to cultivate in the course of such a crisis. We also must include an explanation of the basic strategy that we have been pursuing here in Moscow for a number of decades now.

This is because we have been *greatly* blessed in our community, and so it is absolutely necessary for us to equip ourselves in two areas. We must educate our immigrants, and we must educate the next generation. If we do not do this, then we will be faced with two disasters. The first is what might be called "Californians moving to Texas, but continuing to vote like Californians." The second is the son of a billionaire growing up without ever breaking a sweat, or having any knowledge what having calluses might be like.

Experiencing blessings without understanding the basis of those blessings is like dancing blindfold along the edge of a precipice. As Cotton Mather put it, faithfulness begat prosperity, and the daughter devoured the mother. Or as Moses described Israel's future prosperity and apostasy, Jeshurun waxed fat, and kicked (Deut. 32:15). Moses knew that once you are well into a blessing, it is perilously easy to take it all for granted, and simply to assume that continuation of that blessing is your irrevocable birthright (Deut. 8:1-20). The apostle Paul saw what had happened to the Jews in this thoughtlessness, and warned the Gentile Christians in Rome against committing the very same sin (Rom. 11:19-21). And he issued the same stern warning to the Gentile Christians at Corinth (1 Cor. 10:1-11).

> Under three things the earth trembles; under four it cannot bear up: a slave when he becomes king, and a fool when he is filled

> with food; an unloved woman when she gets
> a husband, and a maidservant when she dis-
> places her mistress. (Prov. 30:21–23, ESV)

There is a pressing temptation, whenever someone unexpectedly comes into great blessing, to react thoughtlessly and glibly, like some cracker redneck who won big at Powerball. We handle it the way a two-year-old would handle a glass of whiskey. Whatever you do, whatever you say, however you think of it, don't be that guy.

A MINISTER'S TASK

One of the things I need to do early on in this small booklet is explain what I think I am up to, and why you should read any further.

The message a minister is appointed to proclaim is the basic gospel message—the life, death, burial and resurrection of Jesus (1 Cor. 15:1-4)—oriented, as it necessarily must be, to the whole counsel of God (Acts 20:27). This is not a message torn out of the Scriptures, but rather a message that is situated at the center of all Scripture.

But the wisdom of God is not placed in our trust so that we may speak it into a void. The preacher is not supposed to learn what he is supposed to say the same way a parrot does, or an answering machine, and then say *that*, regardless of the circumstances. No matter who calls, the answering machine says the same thing. This is not the commission of a minister of the Word.

No. Preachers of the gospel must also be students of the culture they are sent to. A minister must be a student of the Word, but he must also be a student of *men*. He must study them—not just men generally, but the men of his own era, the men to whom he is charged to bring the gospel. When the Lord speaks to each of the angels of the seven churches of Asia, the message for each church is different. Same gospel, different sins, and so a different message applying that gospel.

And men are not to be studied so that the minister might best know how to flatter them. "For *we never came with words of flattery*, as you know, nor with a pretext for greed—God is witness" (1 Thess. 2:5, ESV, emphasis added). Rather, they must be studied because their sins are different, their blind spots vary, and this is why their fortifications against the Spirit of God must be *attacked* differently.

> For though we walk in the flesh, we do not
> war after the flesh: (For the weapons of our

warfare are not carnal, but mighty through
God to the pulling down of strong holds;)
Casting down imaginations, and every high
thing that exalteth itself against the knowledge of God, and bringing into captivity every thought to the obedience of Christ. (2
Cor. 10:3–5)

A man who is charged with pulling down strong-
holds must be a student, therefore, of two things.
He must be a swtudent of the gear he is using, and
he must be a student of the tower he is charged
with toppling. He must know the gospel, and the
Scripture that houses it, and he must also know
the state of the current imaginations, whether
those imaginations are healthy or diseased. He
needs to know where to attach the ropes. This
means that in order to have a true impact, a local
church must understand some of the fundamen-
tal theological issues in play and how they inter-
sect with the large cultural issues of our day.

CHAPTER ONE

OUR CULTURE, WHAT REMAINS OF IT

We are in the midst of a massive religious/political/cultural transformation. But we cannot assume that this is all a downside. God shakes what can be shaken so that what cannot be shaken may remain (Heb. 12:27). This turmoil is rattling things that need to be rattled, and also rattling things that need to be understood, so that they might be defended in wisdom, and not maintained on cruise control.

In the meantime, speaking of traditions, there are no pacifist traditions left. All worthy traditions must be militant in order to survive this time of upheaval.

And in such a time, Christians must be conservative when it comes to everything that the Spirit has accomplished in the history of our civilization. And we must be progressive with regard to all the things He has yet to do.

THE SINFUL SYMPTOMS

It is difficult to make it through the evening news without encountering multiple examples of our contemporary follies—the blood guilt of abortion on demand, the insanity of transgenderism, the idea that more government can save us from the weather, the acceptance of socialist collectivism, the indulgence of snowflakes, the incompetence of modern educators, the epidemic of food guilt, the pandemic of father hunger, and more. The disease lies deep within, but the splotches on the skin are pretty ugly.

Most people understand that something is desperately wrong. Is there any biblical response to it?

THE DISEASE WITHIN

The root of every rebellion (in every culture) must always be identified as pride, and the lust for autonomy. But this central sin manifests itself in different ways in different times, using different methods, concepts, and techniques. Below I have listed some of the ideological tools that are currently being used on us. Please be aware that there are areas of overlap between these.

- *Secularism*—the idea that a culture can be religiously neutral. This is not a nice but difficult goal. Rather, it is an incoherent concept. All cultures serve their gods, and ours is no exception. Our pretense of neutrality does not make us less worshippers, but it does guarantee that we are most confused about our worship;
- *Darwinism*—the idea that we somehow arrived here by ourselves, which makes secularism a scientifically respectable concept. A century or so ago, many Christians thought that we could make our peace with Darwinism. But the bills are now coming due;
- *Egalitarianism*—the idea that bless-

ings for others are tantamount to oppression for me. Egalitarians view everything as a zero sum game—if someone else gets a bigger piece of pie, this necessitates that someone else is going to get a smaller piece. But in the world God made, the pie grows;

• *Value/Fact Distinction*—the idea that "reality" is divisible, and that science is in charge of the "facts," while each individual can invent and tailor his own "values" in any way he pleases;

• *Relativism, Subjectivism, the Despotism of Feelings*—the idea that the world of facts is not the controlling reality. Reality, in other words, is optional;

• *Admiration of the Cool Kids*—the idea that what really matters is copping a pose.

And so some might worry that I am adding "intellectual" requirements to the simple gospel of Christ. Don't worry—it is actually the reverse. You generally need a couple years of grad school before you can *really* buy into any of these mistakes.

Keep in mind that when we answer these challenges in the way we must—in the name of

Jesus Christ—we are *not* supplying Christ as the solution to the problems as posed by these idolatries. He does not give us answers to *their* questions. He gives us His answers to *His* questions. Christ is the one who frees us from these idolatries by toppling all six of them, burning them at the Kidron Brook, crushing them to powder, and scattering the dust on the graves of the people (2 Kings 23:6-7).

CHAPTER TWO

ALTERNATIVE CITY WALLS

The need of the hour is for the Church to help establish a *defined* counterculture. This requires much more than defined denominational boundaries, or sectarian carve-outs. There needs to be a defined center (the *Church*), a defined staging area (the *kingdom*), and a defined mission field (the *world*).

In order to accomplish this, we need brick and mortar to build the alternative city walls. We have been working at this for some decades now in Moscow, and we know how we mix that mortar.

Now one of the key ingredients in that mortar is unrelenting antipathy to the ways of the world. Our danger is that any success in this (what people call "our community") will attract people who love the walls, and the security they provide, but do not like how we lay the bricks. They love the fruit but do not care for the orchard.

They like how the Church works because they are actually assuming the world (at its best) should be able to work that same way. They want to believe that the world is, at bottom, more or less reasonable. They love how different the Church is because they have a hidden assumption that the Church is not all *that* different. This does require some explanation.

> Woe unto you, when all men shall speak well of you! for so did their fathers to the false prophets. But I say unto you which hear, Love your enemies, do good to them which hate you, Bless them that curse you, and pray for them which despitefully use you. (Luke 6:26–28)

Jesus teaches that when we finally have that "good testimony" we have been striving for, we ought immediately to see a red danger light blinking on the dashboard of our sanctification center. Something has gone terribly wrong.

But objections come immediately to mind. We note that some people know how to get everybody to hate them simply by being jerks. Pagans certainly hate one another (Titus 3:3), and that doesn't make the other despised pagan godly. And Peter says that we should rejoice when we are persecuted for the sake of Christ (1 Pet. 4:14, 16), but goes on to add that we must be certain that it really *is* for the sake of Christ and not because we are being what theologians like to call punk-Christians (4:15).

So how can we tell if we are guilty of this false credit that takes as a badge of honor a sign that we are actually being disobedient? The answer is found in Luke 6. What do we read in the next breath?

Those who can take legitimate comfort from the fact that they are slandered are those who can *love* their enemies, *do good* to their haters, *bless* those who curse them, and *pray* for those who are malicious in their mistreatment. They come into your shop to buy something while sneering at it, and so you must give back *scriptural change*.

If you pay them back in their own coin, then this encouragement does not apply. It only applies to those who can do a little jig when they are reviled (Luke 6:23). Those who pick and choose passages from the Bible to encourage them in their selfishness will often find themselves having to pick and choose phrases out of the *same* text.

This passage applies, in other words, to the Christian who is an honest tradesman, a diligent father, a hard-working and cheerful mother, whose children are cheerful and well-loved, and is as friendly as it gets. When a controversy starts, he knows how to conduct himself, but it wasn't his surly face that started the controversy.

A required antipathy to the ways of the world is not exactly an obscure teaching.

> And *I will put enmity* between thee and the woman, and between thy seed and her seed; it shall bruise thy head, and thou shalt bruise his heel. (Gen. 3:15, emphasis added)

This enmity between the "two seeds" cannot be erased, and attempts to erase it are actually attempts to go over to the other side.

> Ye adulterers and adulteresses, know ye
> not that the friendship of the world *is en-*
> *mity with God*? whosoever therefore will
> be a friend of the world *is the enemy of* God.
> (James 4:4, emphasis added)

If you want to be God's adversary, then sim-ply make friends with the world. That's all you have to do. "Yea, and all that will live god-ly in Christ Jesus shall suffer persecution" (2 Tim. 3:12). This means that you *cannot* strive for Christ-likeness in this dark world without bringing down on your head something of what came down on Christ's head. "If the world hate you, ye know that it hated me before it hated you" (John 15:18). So stop acting surprised at things that the Bible talks about *all over the place*. "Marvel not, my brethren, if the world hate you" (1 John 3:13). "And ye shall be hated of all men for my name's sake: but he that endureth to the end shall be saved . . ." (Matt. 10:21–26).

The enmity will end at some point—after you are dead and deep.

Jesus pointed out that *after* prophets are dead and gone, their reputations start to improve. This is because the only manageable prophet is a dead prophet. And if enough time passes, the ungodly start to build memorials to the deceased godly, lining it all with marble (Matt. 23:29). But whenever a *living* Christian leader comes back from a hot engagement at the front, with a couple of arrows through his hat, the careful men are quite willing to offer their critiques. "It would have been far better had you remembered to . . ." It reminds me of Dwight Moody's great comment in response to criticism of his approach to evangelism—"I like my way of doing it better than your way of not doing it."

It also reminds me of Ambrose Bierce's magnificent definition: "REAR, n. In American military matters, that exposed part of the army that is nearest to Congress."[1]

But why, the persistent critics want to know, can't you be more like the saintly men of old, whose marbled tombs grace the avenues of our city? The first thing to recall is that the marvelous city they refer to was not built by the critics, but rather by the criticized.

What "saintly men of old" are they referring to? Perhaps Spurgeon, who was vilified throughout the course of his ministry? Or Augustine, who wrote his famous *Confessions* because he

---

1. *The Devil's Dictionary* (London: Arthur F. Bird, 1906).

was answering a smear campaign that was hindering his ministerial effectiveness? Or like Athanasius who stood *contra mundum*, that world being the *Christian* world, the world of accommodating *bishops*? Examples could be multiplied to the point of being pretty tedious. This is not something that has happened from time to time in history. It is regular enough to be called a *law*.

The principles don't change. The names do. Because the names change, this makes unprincipled people think that *everything* is different now. We are in the 21st century now, distinguished in this respect by being exactly like all the other centuries that came before.

Now remember that in our generation, *feeeelllings!!* are the queen of the land. People don't want to know if a Christian apologist has actually wronged someone else in the course of his ministry. They just want to know if the other guy *felt* wronged. And of course it took about ten minutes for the unbelievers to figure out that you could get most Christians to back off just by saying, *Ow ow ow ow!*

We have managed to get ourselves into a pickup basketball game with the godless, where they all get to call their own fouls, and the fouls that are called on them can only be called by that guy standing on the sidelines, one of the subs for the godless. And we call this striving for fair play. Jesus called it right when He said that the children of light were sometimes a little slow on the uptake (Luke 16:8).

As for the infidels, our central offense is *not* the presence of what I call the "satiric bite." Do not be distracted by what they *call* a foul. They simply call them because it works—we listen to it; we put up with it. In their book, such things are not even an offense at all. Are you serious? They don't care about that. In their understanding, the offense is where the jabs are *aimed*. Remember that these are the people who laugh at the taunting of late night comedians, who host banquet "roasts" that are filled with vile insults, who host parades through all our major cities with floats celebrating vile deeds, and who otherwise sit in the seat of mockers. So why are they so sensitive all of a sudden? Why do they act like snowflakes? It is a *tactic*, and they don't like it when the tactic doesn't work. As the old blues song puts it, "it ain't no fun when the rabbit's got the gun."

When David went out to face Goliath, he was not looking for a dialogue partner.

> This day will the LORD deliver thee into mine hand; and I will smite thee, and take thine head from thee; and I will give the carcases of the host of the Philistines this day unto the fowls of the air, and to the wild beasts of the earth; that all the earth may know that there is a God in Israel. (1 Sam. 17:46)

And when Nehemiah established a great wall that separated the people of God from the unbelievers, the unbelievers did not take it well.

> And I sent messengers unto them, saying, I am doing a great work, so that I cannot come down: why should the work cease, whilst I leave it, and come down to you? Yet they sent unto me four times after this sort; and I answered them after the same manner. Then sent Sanballat his servant unto me in like manner the fifth time with an open letter in his hand; Wherein was written, It is reported among the heathen, and Gashmu saith it, that thou and the Jews think to rebel: for which cause

> thou buildest the wall, that thou mayest be
> their king, according to these words. (Neh.
> 6:3–6)

You really should give up preaching. And blogging. And publishing. And declaring. And challenging. And prophetically denouncing. And why? *Gashmu saith it*. And who is Gashmu? We are not sure exactly, but it distresses us that he is displeased.

CAN YOU PREACH JESUS THAT WAY?

The answer is, of course, to preach Christ. But it needs to be observed that it is not possible for a man to preach Christ while simultaneously ignoring the words of Christ. Preaching Christ means preaching both His words *and* His wounds. You cannot preach the cross, which *is* a scandal, without scandal. There is no such thing as sanitized gospel faithfulness. It doesn't exist, and never has.

Now the Christian Church is unique kind of community in that it is a community built up around scandal. Scandal blows most communities apart, but scandal—the scandal of the cross—is the foundation of all true Christian fellowship. Christ was crucified by all the respectable authorities, and His followers were instructed to tell the story of how that happened down to the end of the world. The Church, like all human institutions in this fallen world, has repeatedly been tempted to drift into "respectability." But this message of the cross lies at the center of our existence, and there are enough antibodies there to fight off every form of a creeping carnal respectability.

But with that said, there is a wrinkle. Over time, more than a few Christian churches drift into a form of organization that is more threatened by scandal than a Christian church really ought to be. And so they pull their skirts away, and begin reacting to the possibility of cross-related scandal in much the same way that ordinary human associations would do. This leads us, necessarily, to the next chapter.

CHAPTER THREE

MEMBERSHIP, LIKE-MINDEDNESS, AND LOYALTY

As we build these new city walls in the midst of a ruined and ruinous old order, we will be attacked in ways that seek to divide us. We will be accused of being cultic, in thrall to charismatic "leaders." But the Scriptures *do* require us to cultivate like-mindedness, and also require us to maintain a solid distinction between things of first importance, things of secondary importance, and things indifferent.

One of the things that modern Christians have a hard time doing right is loyalty. We don't even know how loyalty is supposed to work. We don't understand the spiritual *requirement* of personal allegiance to your church and its leadership, and in addition we have a very poor understanding of what disloyalty actually smells like.

> *Be of the same mind* one toward another. Mind not high things, but condescend to men of low estate. Be not wise in your own conceits. (Rom. 12:16, emphasis added)

As we study this topic, please keep in mind the fact that we are told this same kind of thing *often* (Rom. 15:5-6; 2 Cor. 13:11; Phil. 1:27; 2:2; 1 Pet. 3:8; Phil. 2:20).

As you can see in the text cited above, like-mindedness is a function of humility. It is not necessarily a function of high intellectual attainment. If that is accompanied by pride (as it often is—1 Cor. 8:1), then the opposite of like-mindedness will occur. Never forget that the unity of the Spirit in the bond of peace—which necessarily includes this like-mindedness—is in fact a work of the Spirit. And where the Spirit comes He engenders the fruit of the Spirit, which in their turn contribute to humility, grace, peace, and like-mindedness.

Let us look at membership first.

> Remember them *which have the rule over you,* who have spoken unto you the word of God: whose faith follow, considering the end of their conversation. (Heb. 13:7, emphasis added)

> *Obey them* that have *the rule over you,* and *submit* yourselves: for they watch for your souls, as they that must give account, that they may do it with joy, and not with grief: for that is unprofitable for you. (Heb. 13:17, emphasis added)

These two verses, incidentally, taken together, provide a compelling argument for membership in a local congregation. These individuals have to know the names of the men who rule over them—you cannot obey a nebulous or undefined leadership. And a body of elders cannot render an account for an undefined membership either.

What would you think if you took your taxes to an accountant, and when he gave the package back to you, you asked, "So this is how much I owe?" and he said something like, "Yeah, well, ball park," or, "More or less" while making vague gestures in the air. One thing you want accountants to do is count.

If you don't know who your rulers are, you cannot consider the outcome of their conduct or way of life. And if you don't know who you are responsible for, you cannot watch over their souls. So these two verses, taken together, *require two lists of names*—a list of the elders and a list of the members. Obedience to Scripture at this point is impossible otherwise. Pastors and elders are not allowed to look at their flocks on a distant hillside, as painted by an impressionist at a low point in his game, and while also working with dirty brushes. "Be thou diligent to know the state of thy flocks, and look well to thy herds" (Prov. 27:23). No, giving an account is not limited to mere counting, but it certainly includes counting.

DOCTRINAL REQUIREMENTS?

Our understanding of the doctrinal requirements for church membership follows the historic Presbyterian understanding of it. Our church has adopted the Westminster Confession, but we did not do this to provide our congregation with a doctrinal straitjacket.

What this tells us is what doctrinal framework the saints can expect to hear from the pulpit. It does not tell them what *they* are required to affirm. They are bound to affirm nothing until and unless they see it in the text of Scripture for themselves—but after that, of course honesty requires them to affirm it.

We are a Reformed church, but this means that an Arminian charismatic dispensationalist could join. What we require of our members is a biblical confession that Jesus is Lord, which would mean the basic contents of the Apostles' Creed, and that they agree not to go downtown on the weekends to shoot out the streetlights.

A NARNIAN ILLUSTRATION

No human authority is absolute, and yet at the same time we are taught in Scripture that the authority of lesser authorities is genuine, and that they are to be honored as far as obedience to God allows. This creates a problem, but it is a problem *that God wants us to have*.

Let me begin by noting that—in this as in so many other situations—there is a ditch on both sides of the road. One ditch might be called the "Dear Leader" ditch, which would be an insistence that everyone applaud like they were a spectator at a North Korean missile parade, clapping in sync with the goose-stepping soldiers. That really is cultic.

But in the other ditch we find ornery cussedness, pretending to be valiant for truth, but in the last analysis such persons are loyal only to their own thoughts, opinions, and perspectives. These people are disrespectful, disloyal, and disruptive.

Let us take a look at the fine example of Trumpkin. On the one hand we have stout loyalty.

> "Thimbles and thunderstorms!" cried Trumpkin in a rage. "Is that how you speak to the King? Send me, Sire, I'll go." "But I thought you didn't believe in the Horn, Trumpkin," said Caspian. "No more I do, your Majesty. But what's that got to do with it? I might as well die on a wild goose chase as die here. You are my King. I know the difference between giving advice and

taking orders. You've had my advice, and now it's the time for orders."[2]

Now that's loyalty right there.

But *earlier*, when some Black Dwarfs had suggested the possibility of bringing in a Hag or an Ogre or two to help their cause against Miraz, Trufflehunter objects to that on the basis of what Aslan would think about it. Trumpkin responds to Trufflehunter in a telling way. There are plain limits to loyalty.

> "We should not have Aslan for our friend if we brought in *that* rabble," said Trufflehunter, as they came away from the cave of the Black Dwarfs. "Oh, Aslan!" said Trumpkin, cheerily but contemptuously. "What matters much more is that you wouldn't have me."[3]

Biblical loyalty has limits. But we must emphasize that they are *defined* limits. We don't get to be done with loyalty because we are tired of it, or because it has become inconvenient for us. Rather, Scripture defines what our ultimate

---

2. C.S. Lewis, *Prince Caspian* (New York: Harper Collins, 1951), 92.

3. Ibid., 72.

loyalties must be, and how our subordinate loyalties are to interact.

ACTUAL TEMPTATIONS

As long as we are quoting Lewis, here is a relevant observation from *Screwtape*.

> The game is to have them all running about with fire extinguishers whenever there is a flood, and all crowding to that side of the boat which is already nearly gunwale under."[4]

When it comes to life in our modern congregations, we think we have to guard against mindless conformity when what really threatens our spiritual health is our radical individualism. The Scriptures tell us what we should be laboring for, striving for, and praying for. We are *not* told to work at maintaining independence of thought, although real independence of thought is a good thing. We are not told to build some ecclesiastical variant of academic freedom. We are commanded to strive for like-mindedness, to be of one mind. Our task is assigned, and that is what we should focus on.

---

4. C. S. Lewis, *The Screwtape Letters* (New York: HarperOne, 2001), 138.

Allow me the privilege of translating all of this into modern American English for you. Drink the Kool-Aid. Join the cult. Surrender your independence. Swallow the party line. Go *baaa* like a sheep. Strive for the nirvana of acquiescence.

Modern Christians allow the *Bible* to talk that way about like-mindedness because it is their sacred book and so they are technically stuck with it. But if any Christian leader, anywhere, anytime, *teaches* that obedience and maintaining a teachable spirit are virtues to be cultivated by church members, then that guy is now a hazard with blinking lights all over him. He is clearly power-tripping. "I wrote unto the church: but Diotrephes, who loveth to have the preeminence among them, receiveth us not" (3 John 9). Any authoritative teacher must be a Diotrephes. He is Diotrephes *automatically*. We forget that the apostle John, writing about Diotrephes, was every bit as authoritative (3 John 10).

SO PURSUE CHRIST

Now this means that members of churches have assigned duties of *loyalty* and *obedience*. But what some Christians today believe is that their membership actually requires impudent feedback when they disagree, preferably online. And

I have seen some behavior in that department that, as one of my daughters might put it, makes my eyeballs sweaty.

But people today are nevertheless hungry for true community, and true community is impossible apart from shared values and mores—*like-mindedness*, in other words. But once real community actually starts to form, the attacks on the "cult" will begin. Vulnerable and sophomoric Christians in the community will be taunted—*prove* your independence. Whatever your leader asks for, vote *no*, drag your feet, raise a stink, and put some daylight between yourself and that guy. As if you could establish independence by always finding the North Star, and always sailing south by it. But *that's* not real independence.

True independence of mind exists where there can be disagreement without demonizing the one you differ with. And this cannot be done unless you let Scripture instruct you on how to distinguish things that are of first importance and things that are of much lesser importance.

Remember that unity and like-mindedness are a function of being apprehended by, and apprehending, *Christ*. He is the one in whom every joint and ligament joins (Eph. 4:16).

CHAPTER FOUR

THE MEANING OF LOVE
AND JUSTICE

T he central difficulty with the great idol
of the collective, the false god of stat-
ism, is that we have wanted to substi-
tute the word of man for the Word of God. We
want to define love according to our own lights.
We have wanted to define justice without reference to biblical law, and this then makes us want
to choose between individualism and collectivism. And then, because we have been thrown
into a realm where might determines right, the
collective always wins.

Within the Christian body, there is an assigned place for each individual, and there is a
defined reality that is the corporate body, made
up of all the individuals. This reality was created
by God, and is objective. That means that we
must conform to it, and stop trying to make it
conform to our feelings. When we learn this les-
son, we have learned both love and justice.

We are *individuals* saved by grace, bound together in a mystical *body*. This has been done
in accordance with the Scriptures, which means
that love and justice are defined from *outside the
world*. And it also means the Church provides
the only genuine alternative to the chaos of the
one and the many in the unbelieving world.

> Owe no man any thing, but to love one
> another: for he that loveth another hath
> fulfilled the law. For this, Thou shalt not
> commit adultery, Thou shalt not kill, Thou
> shalt not steal, Thou shalt not bear false
> witness, Thou shalt not covet; and if there
> be any other commandment, it is brief-
> ly comprehended in this saying, namely,
> Thou shalt love thy neighbour as thyself.

> Love worketh no ill to his neighbour: there-
> fore love is the fulfilling of the law. (Rom.
> 13:8–10)

A community like those we seek to build should be bound together by love. Sounds great, but what do we mean exactly? Our bonds to one another need to be *stronger* than the bonds of debtor/creditor (v. 8). If we love the other person, then that means we have fulfilled the law. Paul then mentions the seventh, sixth, eighth, ninth, and tenth commandments, in that order, and says that they are all *comprehended* in this one commandment, "Love your neighbor as yourself" (Lev. 19:18). The word rendered as *comprehended* is a verb that comes from the root *kephale*, meaning *head* (v. 9). Paul then tells us why. Love works no evil to its neighbor, and this is why love is the fulfillment of the law (v. 10). Love, in short, refuses to perpetrate injustice, and justice is always defined by the law of God, which in turn is shaped by the character of God Himself—and remember that God *is* love (1 John 4:8). Put all these together, and meditate on these identities. God is love, love is the law ... and so we may conclude that the law is not an adversary to love.

Remember also the context of this passage from Romans 13, and that chapter divisions were not in the original. Do not retaliate personally against injustice (Rom. 12:17). It is not that vengeance is wrong, but rather that vengeance is the *Lord's* (Rom. 12:19). Show *grace* in your own name (Rom. 12:21). Since vengeance and wrath belong to God, He has the authority to deputize His own agents (or deacons) of wrath, which He has done in the civil magistrate (Rom. 13:1-4). So the love that is enjoined in Rom. 13:8-10 is not in an adversarial relationship with the facts of hard justice. It is possible *because* of hard justice. The hard justice is one of the premises from which Paul argues to get to his exhortation for us to give ourselves over to love. Hard teaching creates tender hearts. Tender teaching creates hard hearts. The jackhammer of the Word breaks up our hard hearts. The feather duster of the Word leaves our hard hearts just where they were.

INJUSTICE IS THEREFORE LOVELESSNESS

Injustice is sin. And the apostle John defines sin for us in a very succinct way. "Everyone who makes a practice of sinning also practices lawlessness; sin is lawlessness" (1 John 3:4, ESV).

Sin is lawlessness. That's it; that's the heart of it. But what is it to keep the law from the heart? Scripture describes *that* as love. And so what does it mean to love someone? It means to treat them lawfully from the heart.

Note that this excludes a mere ticking of boxes. The emphasis needs to be *on the heart*. Jesus teaches us this explicitly. "Thou blind Pharisee, cleanse first that which is within the cup and platter, that the outside of them may be clean also" (Matt. 23:26). Cleansing the outside of the cup doesn't get the inside clean. But when the inside is clean, what happens? Jesus says, "that the outside may be clean also." Clean the outside, and you have a (partially) cleaned outside. Clean the inside, and you get a clean inside and outside both.

THE GREAT CLASH

Earlier in this book, I said that one of the great enemies of our day is "relativism, subjectivism, the despotism of feelings." And by this I meant "the idea that the world of facts is not the controlling reality. Reality, in other words, is optional." We have been taught—*ad nauseam* we have been taught—that love is what you *feel*. When the feeling wanes or goes away, as the theory goes, so has the love. This has been the source of untold misery in the world. According to the ethical system of snowflakes and SJWs, injustice is defined by whether or not it hurts someone's feelings.

But in the biblical framework, when your feelings start to wander off, love looks up with a sharp maternal gleam in her eye and says, *"Get back here."* In a biblical framework, you and all your feeling are like a first-grade teacher taking her whole class to some busy downtown museum, and because she *loves* them, every last one of them is on a neon-colored leash.

COVENANT BONDS

As we talk about true Christian community, which is based on *koinonia* fellowship, we have to begin with the nature of covenant commitments. This applies to marriage and family, it applies to membership in the church, and it applies to the rest of life also. I am going to ask you to bear with a few illustrations, but they all line up with what a wise Puritan once said about marriage. "First he chooses his love, and then he loves his choice."

If you go down in the basement of a house, you will likely be able to find cold concrete in straight lines. Let us call it cold *covenant* concrete—a bunch of very *unsentimental* concrete. Then go up into the living room, and you will there find curtains, warm colors, cushions, sofas, carpet, and so on. This is where you live, and it is what makes living there enjoyable, but it *cannot* be the foundation of the house. Roll up the carpet, mound all the cushions, throw the curtains on top of it, and then try to situate a stud wall on top of *that*.

Or imagine you discipline your emotions the same way some folks discipline their kids. Some people are so disordered in this that they have come to believe that if someone's "children" are not unruly hellions, then this must mean that they don't even *have* kids. No, they have kids, but their kids *mind*. They obey. They *behave*. We like to describe self-controlled people as "unemotional," but what we really mean is that their emotions are not half-civilized yard apes on a sugar rush. And by the way, before the wrong people start commending themselves for how "unemotional" they are, I would remind them that anger is an emotion.

Covenant vows, covenant oaths don't move. They are to be the foundation. Your feelings and sentiments *do* move. What happens if you make them the foundation? When they go up and down, the whole house goes up and down—like living in a volatile earthquake zone.

Foundations *matter*. This is the Lord's express teaching.

> Therefore whosoever heareth these sayings of mine, and doeth them, I will liken him unto a wise man, which built his house upon a rock: And the rain descended, and the floods came, and the winds blew, and beat upon that house; and it fell not: for it was founded upon a rock. And every one that heareth these sayings of mine, and doeth them not, shall be likened unto a foolish man, which built his house upon the sand: And the rain descended, and the floods came, and the winds blew, and beat upon that house; and it fell: and great was the fall of it. (Matt. 7:24–27)

And recall the three governments mentioned earlier—the family is the ministry of health, education, and welfare. The Church is the ministry of grace and peace. The civil magistrate is the ministry of justice. But the (non-institutional) government that supports and makes possible all three of these is *self-government*.

PUT ON YOUR JESUS COAT

Because we are forgiven by God through Christ (Eph. 4:32), so it is possible for us to be exhorted to imitate Christ (1 Pet. 2:21). But we are to imitate the whole process. Jesus did what He did for the joy that was set before Him (Heb. 12:2), and because of His obedience true joy is a possibility. But Jesus did not go to the cross on an emotional high. The greatest act of love that was ever offered up to God was the death of Christ on the cross (Rom. 5:8), and Jesus tried to get out of it (Matt. 26:39). But *His* house was not built on the cushions, and so it is that we are saved. His love for you had a more sure foundation than that. What would have happened to you and to me if in the garden Christ had obeyed His feelings instead of His Father?

So put on Christ (Rom. 13:14; Gal. 3:27). Put on your Jesus coat. And make sure you put your arms through *both* sleeves.

CHAPTER FIVE

LITTLE PLATOONS

T rue community is something that develops as the result of interwoven relationships, multiple tightly-knit relationships, and that requires an ethos of hospitality. The modern temptation to individualism is a far cry from being a libertarian answer to collectivism, and is rather one of the central reasons why collectivism has swallowed up so much.

Enslaved societies are atomistic, while free societies are molecular. When every individual is a solitary BB, and you dump all the BBs into a sack—we shall call the sack "the state"—you

find that it has all the solidity of a bean bag
chair. At some point it occurs to the powers that
be that it would be to their advantage to encourage sexual license, and to legalize pot, which is
a move that greases all the BBs. Individuals are
in no position effectively to resist the encroach-
ments of the state.

For that we need Edmund Burke's little pla-
toons. Subordinate loyalties give society a molecular rigidity and structure. This means there
must be a profound commitment to the covenant of marriage, a real hostility to divorce, a
true dedication to bringing up the kids in the
nurture and admonition of the Lord, and so on.
But this by itself, even though it is molecular,
is not yet complex enough. In order for real
Christian communities to grow and develop,
there has to be more. There has to be a real understanding of hospitality.

LAYERS OF HOSPITALITY

In the modern world, hospitality generally refers
to the work of the hotel industry—the world of
innkeepers. Without casting any shade on the
importance of this—having been in really good

hotels and really poor ones—it is not where the center of hospitality should be.

We can begin with our responsibility to strangers. In the ancient world, the duty to extend hospitality to strangers was sacrosanct, which is why the treatment of Lot's visitors by the residents of Sodom was so appalling (Gen. 19), as well as the treatment of the unnamed Levite and his concubine at the hands of the men of Gibeah (Judg. 19). We should also mention in passing that the behavior of Lot and the Levite was also appalling, while at the same time noting that their behavior makes no sense without a backdrop of a strict code of hospitality with regard to strangers.

So modern Christian hospitality should make room for the stranger, for the true guest, for the person who is just visiting your town. This would include traveling missionaries, or refugees from some blue state. They are people you are not necessarily close to, and you actually have no reason to suppose you will ever see them again. It is still important. It means that you are keeping your hospitality muscles in good shape.

"Do not neglect to show hospitality to strangers, for thereby some have entertained angels unawares" (Heb. 13:2, ESV).

This element is on the list when considering the qualifications for women to be added to roster of those that the church supports. Hospitality most certainly includes showing grace to the traveler.

> Let not a widow be taken into the number under threescore years old, having been the wife of one man. Well reported of for good works; if she have brought up children, if she have lodged strangers, if she have washed the saints' feet, if she have relieved the afflicted, if she have diligently followed every good work. (1 Tim. 5:9-10)

For those in a position to do so, it could be good to build a guest room or cottage that enables you to extend that particular grace. This is what the Shunammite woman did for Elisha (2 Kings 4:9-10).

A related category would be those who are less fortunate, or down and out.

> But when thou makest a feast, call the poor, the maimed, the lame, the blind: And thou

shalt be blessed; for they cannot recompense thee: for thou shalt be recompensed at the resurrection of the just. (Luke 14:13–14)

Jesus here is getting at the heart of how hospitality can go wrong, when it goes wrong. There are obvious limits here—if you have little kids you don't want to fill up your house with meth addicts—but at the same time we cannot let our understanding of the obvious limits become something that trumps an obvious text.

There is a way of entertaining that gives your guests a show, or a good time, or a magnificent array of new taste sensations in their mouths, all of it designed to make you look good. It is a glorified way of showing off. You put on the Ritz for all your acquaintances, and the way the game is played means that at some point they have to invite you back and try to outdo you. You get two fantastic meals for the price of one.

But there is another way, the way of hospitality, in which you give *yourself*.

In one world, the gifts are given *instead* of yourself. In the other world, the world God is fashioning through us, the gifts are tokens or chips that represent something else, and that something else is the giving of the person. Some give gifts so that they don't have to give themselves—like some kind of extortion payment. Others give gifts as a representation of themselves.

If you show hospitality to those who cannot pay you back, this gets you in shape to show that same kind of hospitality to those who live in community with you—with those who could pay you back, but you were no longer thinking of that. We are building up to the need to weave a true community together by means of having each other in your homes. But in order to do this in a way that actually builds community, you absolutely have to mortify that internal bookkeeper that meticulously counts how many times you invited and how many times you have been invited. Paul says that we are to provide for "the necessity of saints; *given to hospitality*" (Rom. 12:13, emphasis added).

This sort of thing is simply assumed as part and parcel of Christian community. Paul says that Christian leaders are to be selected with this particular trait in mind: "A bishop then must be blameless, the husband of one wife, vigilant, sober, of good behaviour, given to hospitality, apt to teach" (1 Tim. 3:2). "For a bishop must be blameless, as the steward of God; not selfwilled, not soon angry, not given to wine, no striker, not given to filthy lucre; *but a lover of hospitality*, a lover of good men, sober, just, holy, temperate" (Titus 1:8, emphasis added).

Given to hospitality. *Lover* of hospitality. This is a big deal. Christian leaders are not the ones doing this so that others won't have to. They are rather to be the ones setting the pitch for the whole choir. They are to be hospitable in such a way that the congregation can consider the outcome of their way of life, and imitate them in it (Heb. 13:7).

There are obvious temptations that come with hospitality. Let us just say that not all guests are equally thoughtful, or grateful, or whatever it is they should be. This is why Peter has to tell us that mumbling under our breath is no way to be dishing up the platters. "Use hospitality one to another without grudging" (1 Pet. 4:9). Hospitality is not easy. If it were easy, everyone would be doing it.

THE LORD WILL REPAY

I said above that we must mortify our internal hospitality bookkeeper. But there I was speaking of our tracking of all our horizontal accounts. We are supposed to give without specific regard for what we might be getting from those we have given to. However, we are supposed to look to God for the return.

"He that hath pity upon the poor lendeth unto the Lord; And that which he hath given will he pay him again" (Prov. 19:17).

There are many ways in which the Lord will repay us through this. One of them is the growth of true Christian community. As we extend this kind of love, the kind of love that has our brothers and sisters in our homes without any sense of reciprocal obligation, the Lord is engaged in weaving a tight fabric, the fabric of genuine fellowship, genuine community, genuine *koinonia*.

CHAPTER SIX

OUTLANDISH YEARS

We have all been witnesses, up close and personal, to a pretty outlandish last couple of years. The tides have behaved the way they always do, and the sunsets continue to be glorious, and the meadowlarks carry on in accord with all their usual customs. But all over the world, in country after country, a very large number of people, the ones running everything, have simultaneously lost their grip.

The subject matter from issue to issue has varied some—from black lives mattering, to young people marching for socialism, to COVID lock downs—but the overarching and unifying theme is that everybody appears to have lost their minds. People know how to choose sides. And they know how to appeal to scientists who support whatever it is they think they know. And they know how to repeat the current talking points. But what they don't know how to do is *think*.

So take three instances at random. A young white college sophomore throws a Molotov cocktail that burns down a black-owned deli, and he does this because he wants to register his deep dissatisfaction with the police treatment of blacks in that city. Or another person, as timid as they come, is out for a walk on a bike path, two miles out of town, all by herself, and she is wearing a mask. Or someone else thinks that it can cost two dollars to get a gallon of milk to market, but also thinks that we can make the greedster grocer sell it for a buck fifty, and yet still have milk on the shelf. What do these, and countless other instances, have in common? What they all have in common is that these people received a lousy education.

As we watch this great parade of duncical folly every night on the news, one thought should come back to haunt us with every fresh insult to right reason. And that thought should be, "Who *educated* these people?" And the follow-up question should be, "And why haven't they been sacked?"

Who taught these people what being a normal human being is supposed to look like? Because they are not hitting it.

GOD IS NOT MOCKED

We have it on good authority that we cannot harvest figs from thorn bushes (Luke 6:44). The kind of seed you put in the ground has a great deal to do with what kind of crop comes up at you out of the ground (Gal. 6:7).

Rendering general by induction, we may infer that it is also not possible to gather pink grapefruit from your juniper bushes, or pine nuts from your tomato plants, or lemons from your box hedge. Pursuing the analogy relentlessly, we may also surmise that you cannot send your child to a culinary school and expect to get back a mechanical engineer. You cannot send them to art school, and wonder why your son never became a doctor like you wanted. You can't pay for law school, and then be surprised when an attorney eventually shows up. We often act astonished when we have no right whatsoever to be surprised in any way. We say, wide-eyed with Aaron, that all we did was put in a bunch of gold, and "out came this calf" (Exod. 32:24). That has to rank as one of the lamest excuses in the Bible, and here we are, still using it.

All we did was put in hundreds of billions of dollars, and out came this misbegotten culture. How could this have happened? We are frankly at a loss.

And lest I be accused of being too oblique in the point I am seeking to make, you cannot send all the Christian kids off to be educated in a school system that is riddled with rank unbelief, shot through with relativism, and diseased with perverse sexual fantasies, and then wonder at the results you get. And why are you not allowed to wonder about it? Because God is not mocked.

EARLY WARNING INDICATORS

Decades ago there were Christian writers warning about the consequences for those Christians who undertook the novel project of planting morning glory and going out months later to harvest the wheat into their barns. It is not as though we weren't warned about this. I know that I have been writing about this problem for decades. And as Voddie Baucham recently put it, "We cannot continue to send our children to Caesar for their education and be surprised when they come home as Romans."[5]

I do want to do this politely and graciously, but there is room in Scripture for the occasional "I told you so."

"But after long abstinence Paul stood forth in the midst of them, and said, Sirs, ye should have hearkened unto me, and not have loosed from Crete, and to have gained this harm and loss" (Acts 27:21).

But to compound the problem, the warnings actually began much earlier.

Back in the 19th century, writing against the public school system *then*, when that school system was still overtly Protestant and evangelical, R.L. Dabney said that "Christians must prepare themselves then for the following results: all Bibles, prayers and catechisms will ultimately be driven out of the schools."[6] We look at that and say, "There used to be *catechisms* in the schools?"

---

5. *Family Driven Faith* (Wheaton, IL: Crossway, 2007), 200.

6. *On Secular Education*, ed. Douglas Wilson (Moscow, ID: Canon Press, 1996), 28.

I started school back in the fifties, and I can still remember praying in government schools, but I don't remember any catechisms. They were exiled much earlier.

A.A. Hodge of Princeton, also in the 19th century, called the shot in this way.

> It is capable of exact demonstration that if every party in the State has the right of excluding from the public schools whatever he does not believe to be true, then he that believes most must give way to him that believes least, and then he that believes least must give way to him that believes absolutely nothing, no matter in how small a minority the atheists or agnostics may be. It is self-evident that on this scheme, if it is consistently and persistently carried out in all parts of the country, the United States system of national popular education will be the most efficient and wide instrument for the propagation of Atheism which the world has ever seen.[7]

---

7. *Popular Lectures on Theological Themes* (Philadelphia: Presbyterian Board of Education, 1887), 281.

And then in the middle of the 20th century, C.S. Lewis gave us these prescient words in his great tract on the necessary consequences of relativistic education:

> In a sort of ghastly simplicity we remove the organ and demand the function. We make men without chests and expect of them virtue and enterprise. We laugh at honour and are shocked to find traitors in our midst. We castrate and bid the geldings be fruitful.[8]

And so here we are, right on schedule. It turns out that, however you might wish otherwise, you eventually wind up wherever it was you were going. If you get on the plane to Chicago, and I would ask you to follow me closely here, you are going to *land in Chicago*. We are now arriving where a godless education must necessarily go. The public schools in America were not secular, they were godless. The public schools in America were not neutral, they were godless. The public schools in America were not even agnostic, they were godless. Lot moved to Sodom, apparently because his wife wanted to be near

8. *The Abolition of Man* (1944; New York: HarperCollins, 2001), 26.

the malls, but he was then somehow vexed by the behavior of the Sodomites.

AGAIN, THE MANDATE

God requires His people to bring up their covenant children in an environment dominated by the Word of God. When we walk along the road, when we lie down, when we rise up (Deut. 6:4-9). Christian fathers are instructed to bring their children up in the *paideia* of the Lord (Eph. 6:4). And if man does not live by bread alone, but by every word that proceeds from the mouth of God (Matt. 4:4), then it follows that boys and girls need to be *instructed* in every word that proceeds from the mouth of God. These things are not optional.

And neither do they happen all by themselves. The passage in Deuteronomy 6 contains the great Shema, Israel's great statement of faith, a statement which leads directly into the greatest commandment in the entire Bible.

"Hear, O Israel: The Lord our God is one Lord: And thou shalt love the Lord thy God with all thine heart, and with all thy soul, and with all thy might" (Deut. 6:4–5).

These words are contained in the middle of a passage on the importance of bringing up your children under the Word of God. It is the beating heart of a passage that is all about Christian education. And thou shalt teach them diligently unto thy children, and thou shalt talk about them *all the time* (Deut. 6:7). This is no peripheral issue, and so where do great apostasies—like the one we are experiencing right now—come from? They come from not doing this. They arise from disobedience.

America has cancer bad, and what would be our disease-ridden lymph nodes? The answer to that question is pretty plain, at least for those willing to repent of the ongoing denial and look straight at the MRI. The answer is our godless educational system, K-12, which is then augmented and brought to a corrupt fruition by our Christless system of higher education. So if you want to get more of what you are getting, go ahead and keep on doing what you are doing.

But at least have the decency to stop complaining about what the harvesters keep bringing in from the fields. Who planted that crop in the first place?

NO CHRISTIAN COMMUNITY WITHOUT
CHRISTIAN EDUCATION

Without a comprehensive system of Christian education, it is possible for *sects* to exist, and it is also possible, for a time, to maintain an anemic denominational presence. But in order to have a flourishing Christian community, it is necessary for the children of that community to have a shared experience of godly education.

This is one of the central reasons why we have been blessed with a functioning Christian community here in Moscow. Just within Christ Church, we have hundreds of school-aged children, and approximately 95% of them are receiving a thoroughly Christian education. And there are multiple education options for parents to choose from—from homeschooling, to Logos Online, to Kepler Education, to White Horse Hall co-op, to Veritas Press Online, to Jubilee School, to Logos School, and so on. Not only is it the case that Christian kids in our town (overwhelmingly) are receiving a Christian education, but it is also the case that a significant percentage of all children in our entire town are receiving a Christian education. This is transformational. And because of growth and demand, the Logos School Board recently made the decision to build a school district.

An alternative culture must begin as a subculture, but that subculture must have a robust immune system. And if that growing alternative culture is to be Christian, there must be a dogged commitment to the centrality of true Christian education. Education is one of the central instruments given to us by God for the establishment and perpetuation of a culture. And if we want the culture to be believing, then the education that feeds into it must be believing.

And no, this does not leave out the gospel. We deny that education can be any kind of a savior. The secularists believe that their education has saving powers, but we do not. Education is no savior. But because we believe the gospel is a world-transforming gospel, we believe that education will be saved. Along with everything else we do, education can be transformed by the blood of Christ, and will be one of His instruments toward the sanctification of Christian culture.

CHAPTER SEVEN

HUGUENOT HUSTLE

According to Scripture, a spiritual man is one who walks in step with the Spirit in this material world (Gal. 5:16). A spiritual man is not an ethereal man, or a wispy man, or a semi-transparent man. A spiritual man is never a *worldly* man (1 John 2:15), but he most certainly is a down-to-earth man. Worldly and practical are not the same thing. While there *have* been people who were so heavenly-minded they were no earthly good, it generally runs the other way. The people who have done the most earthly good have often been the most heavenly-minded. How could deep and intelligent love for ultimate wisdom incapacitate a person? "Seest thou a man diligent in his business? He shall stand before kings; He shall not stand before mean men" (Prov. 22:29). "Do you see a man skillful in his work? He will stand before kings; he will not stand before obscure men" (Prov. 22:29, ESV).

The Bible teaches us that cream rises. This is not because cream has anything to boast of, but rather because of how God created and governs His world. We can plant and water, but God is the one who gives the increase (1 Cor. 3:6-7). Cream rises because of the blessing of God. The point is to seek the blessings of *being* cream, and then secondarily, after that, seeking the blessing that comes to cream. You never want to strive to be skim milk, and yet somehow rise like cream.

And of course, having received such blessings, we are to boast—but we are only to boast in the Lord (1 Cor. 1:31; 2 Cor. 10:17). What do you have that you did not receive as a gift? And if as a gift, then why do you boast as though it were not a gift (1 Cor. 4:7)?

So it is a grace and a gift from God to *excel* in your work. It is another gift from God to reap the benefits of excelling in your work. Though they usually go together (but not *always*), the two must not be confused, and the order of the two must never be reversed. Doing this will enable us to keep our priorities right where they are supposed to be: "A good name is rather to be chosen than great riches, and loving favour rather than silver and gold" (Prov. 22:1).

VOCATION

One of the great accomplishments of the Reformation was the restoration of the idea of *calling* or *vocation* in every lawful endeavor. This abolished the old sacred/secular hierarchy, where it was assumed that if you were *really* sold out for Jesus you would be in a nunnery, or some other place that was equally high-minded. Being a merchant was kind of a tragic necessity, but *somebody* had to bring in the tithes.

Unfortunately, this medieval mistake is creeping back in, having made great inroads in the evangelical world. What do people who are "sold out for Jesus" do now? We now call it "full time Christian work." But what other kind is there? Part time Christians are not the converted ones. According to this unhappy assumption, if you don't enlist in the Navy Seals for Jesus (NSJ), then you can always go into architecture, where you try to pay down some of the guilt for being such a partial Christian by giving donations to the real Christians.

But the doctrine of God's sovereignty and Christ's universal lordship over all things means that we need to put down this idea for good. If you are a faithful Christian, walking in the will of God, then God is advancing the kingdom of His Son through your film-editing, back hoe-operating, diaper-changing, book-writing, music-composing, lawn-mowing, classroom-teaching, study-group organizing, and sermon-preparing. *All* of it is in the palm of God's hand. Remember—all of Christ for all of life. When we say all of life, we mean *all of life*.

Having said this, one caution is in order. Until the resurrection, whenever we are given an understanding of anything, it will be possible to sin with it. The elimination of the old sacred/secular hierarchy was entirely a good thing, having the effect of bringing the authority of Christ to bear on every lawful pursuit. But the law of diminishing returns can kick in, meaning that when everything is sacred, then nothing is.

Affirming the sacralization of all lawful activities *can* be the first step in the secularization of all our activities. So we have to watch our step. We have to remember to keep Christ at the center.

NOT KIDDING YOURSELF

But in all of these endeavors, the biblical pattern is clear. First the planting, then the harvest (1 Cor. 3:6). First the race, then the medals ceremony (1 Cor. 9:24). First the cross, then the crown (1 Cor. 9:25). First the death, then the resurrection (Rom. 6:4).

> "For I say, through the grace given unto me, to every man that is among you, not to think of himself more highly than he ought to think; but to think soberly, according as God hath dealt to every man the measure of faith." (Rom. 12:3)

Because we live in such a flattering age, too many Christians have come to think that successful entrepreneurship is their necessary birthright, and all they have to do is be energetic enough to scoop up the rewards, preferably in cash. And we try to sanctify the attitude that James describes as evil boasting, and we try to sanctify it with how we sought out "the will of God" beforehand.

> "Go to now, ye that say, To day or to morrow we will go into such a city, and continue there a year, and buy and sell, and get gain: Whereas ye know not what shall be on the morrow. For what is your life? It is even a vapour, that appeareth for a little time, and then vanisheth away. For that ye ought to say, If the Lord will, we shall live, and do this, or that." (James 4:13–15)

Because we live in an age of rootless entitlement, we have far too many Christians believing that the world, or their employer, or the government, somehow owes them a living. So not only are they lazy, they are also lazy and entitled. And, to apply the old proverb to them, it could be raining porridge and they'd have forgotten their bowl.

In the days of the Huguenots, there was a saying in France that ran "as honest as a Huguenot." How long do you think it will be before Americans start saying "as honest as an evangelical?" I am not talking about whether it ever happens or not. I am talking about whether it happens so much, so often, and so character-istically that it becomes *proverbial*.

When it comes to business transactions, we need to have a lot more of "do all things to the glory of God," and a lot less of "Christians aren't perfect, just forgiven."

PEACE AND PURITY

When you are engaged, as we are, in seeking to build true Christian community, the first thing that will happen is that an *economy* will start to take shape. And this means, in its turn, that disputes will arise. Most of the gnarly disputes will be about business or finances. This is borne out in my experience, and in line with a survey we sent out to the members of our church community. We asked, for example, how many of them had had business deals with fellow church members go south on them, and more than a few had.

Test your heart first. When you are think-ing about a business opportunity with another member of the church, ask yourself this kind of question *first*. If your first thought is that be-cause so-and-so is a fellow church member he might cut you a deal, then I would plead with you as your pastor to go do business with the pagans. You'll fit in better there. That's how you can best maintain the peace and purity of the church. How many Christians think something like this? *"Ooo*—he has that little fish in his shop window. I think I'll add 10% to whatever he invoices. After all, he's a *brother*."

And when the attitude is right, there is another thing I would ask you to include. Too many Christians think that regeneration, or good intentions, or having a nice personality will somehow make your memory perfect, or will prevent you from getting hit by a truck. Suppose you get hit by that truck, and your heirs and your partners' heirs are all trying to figure out what that handshake fifteen years ago meant. So *write it down*. This does not make you suspicious and unloving. God loves us perfectly, and *He* still wrote it down.

Not only that, but neither does regeneration magically bestow craft competence. Your salvation is by grace through faith, lest anyone should boast (Eph. 2:8-9). But kids, your grade point average does not work that way. Adults, neither does your business work that way. Your vocation in the world is found in the *next* verse.

"For we are his workmanship, created in Christ Jesus unto good works, which God hath before ordained that we should walk in them" (Eph. 2:10). And good works here most manifestly includes *good work*.

Good work is work. Even though the grace of God underlies all things, including all our work, our work remains *work*. Your ability to carry a load of bricks over to the build site is ultimately the grace of God, but the actual carrying is work. The bricks are not moved before you get there "by grace through faith."

DOING BUSINESS WITH BROTHERS

You should go into every business relationship with a brother looking to *give* something additional, rather than trying to *get* something additional. Don't expect discounts because you are a brother. Try, when possible, to give something additional because he's a brother. And when someone in the church is doing business with you, you are not responsible for whether or not they are observing this. And if you decide to stop using the services of a brother it may be because of ordinary reasons (price, distance, etc.), slipshod or substandard workmanship, or unethical work (*biblically* defined). For the first, no explanation is necessary. Just go your way. If the person asks, tell them. For the second, you must tell your brother about your concerns. If you have done so, then it is legitimate to express those concerns to others, if they seek or need your recommendation on this brother's work. If he installed your cabinets upside down, it is not "gossip" to say so when someone asks for a recommendation. For the third scenario, you must follow the pattern given in Matthew 18.

Being a member of the same church does not entitle you to free consulting services. When you ask questions of a brother in business, it should only be in order to determine whether or not you need his services, and not an attempt to get his services without paying for them. Avoid making anyone "set up shop" at church or fellowship events.

At a fellowship event, you can ask questions about "when would be a good time to call about thus and such?" But even here, be sensitive. When you call, after you have asked a few questions about whether or not the services are necessary, you are on the threshold of imposing on a brother. This means that after the first few minutes, you should expect the meter to be running (and should say so). If the person you are talking to does not charge you that is his business. But you should expect a bill as soon as you get to the point of using his expertise.

Remember some professions are more vulnerable to this kind of imposition than others. Low risk: MRI technicians, librarians. Medium risk: teachers, guys with tools and pick-up trucks. High risk: medical doctors, auto mechanics, veterinarians, realtors.

Beware of the egalitarianism which says that it is all right to do this to what you consider "high income" professions. Don't assume that someone "doesn't mind" because you have been doing this to him for years. He just has better manners than you do.

Wives, do not do an end run around your husband. If he has said that you are not going to spend any money on whatever it is, you should not try to get the service without spending any money. This just turns one sin into two.

In all things, apply the Golden Rule. Ask yourself what would be a temptation to you in your profession, and then don't do that to other people in theirs.

THE NEXT LEVEL UP

In addition to these principles, we also want to anticipate our next level of challenges, as brothers go into business partnerships together, as they provide investments for start-ups, and as they provide loans to one another. Every member of our church promises to pursue the purity and peace of the body in their behavior, and we would like every member of the church doing significant business with one another to understand that the following constitutes our understanding of what is entailed in pursuing peace and purity in the realm of business. It is too often the case that we follow Christ when pocket change is involved, but dismiss the demands of discipleship when real money starts to alter our exegesis.

First, taking a business dispute between brothers before the unbelieving civil magistrate is simply out of the question (1 Cor. 6:1-8). If a dispute between members grows past the point of them being able to resolve it, the elders should appoint a committee of qualified brothers to mediate the dispute. If mediation does not resolve the difficulty, the elders should require Christian arbitration. If that arbitration is refused or defied, the church elders move to church discipline.

Second, no one in the body should loan or invest any amount of money that they are not fully and cheerfully prepared to lose. When money is loaned, the Lord *requires* that it be loaned from an open palm (Luke 6:34). When money is invested (and investments are not loans), it is the nature of investments to sometimes go south. "Like an archer who wounds everyone is one who hires a passing fool or drunkard (Prov. 26:10, ESV). Or, as George Herbert once said, "He that sends a fool, means to follow him."[9]

CHRIST OR MAMMON

If you give yourselves to the pursuit of Mammon, it will do nothing but suck you dry. If Christ gives Himself to you, and you surrender yourself in response, the opposite thing happens: "He that believeth on me, as the scripture hath said, out of his belly shall flow rivers of living water"

---

9. George Herbert, *Jacula Prudentium, or Outlandish Proverbs* (London: T. Maxey for T. Garthwait, 1651), 4.

(John 7:38). "The liberal soul shall be made fat: and he that watereth shall be watered also himself" (Prov. 11:25).

This spirit of grace and generosity does not take Mammon out of your hands, but it most certainly takes you out of Mammon's hands. And while Mammon remains a snake, the Lord promised that we could handle serpents without harm (Mark 16:18). But apart from the sovereign grace of God, *you cannot keep money from doing what money always does.*

But Christ—in whose hands you are—*can* keep money from doing what money always does. What is impossible for man is always possible with God. But this only happens if the *crucified and risen* Lord is Lord of your bank account.

CHAPTER EIGHT

SEXUAL SANITY

We are living in a time of sexual bedlam, sexual madness. The frenzy that has captured the Western world has many manifestations—open marriages, pornography, same sex mirage, robo-sex, trannies, and worse. My point in mentioning them is not to get into all these deviations in order to attack or refute them point by point. My point is to acknowledge that we are surrounded by all of this kind of thing, and in that context declare the only alternative to the madness, which is faithful Christian monogamy, and to highlight Scripture's idea of what constitutes a faithful sexual testimony. Because Christian culture is human, then human sexuality is going to occupy a central place in it. This is not central the way sex-obsession is central to a porn addict, but rather central the way eggs are an essential part of making an omelet. It is not a matter of thinking about sex all day and night, but rather recognizing how the marital sexual union is one of God's basic instruments for populating His Heaven with immortal saints.

It is not the case that we are now living in a time when sexual standards are violated by many—they have *always* been violated by many. What we are dealing with is a loss of sexual sanity on the part of our culture generally. We have always had hypocrisy. But to get rid of the double standards and hypocrisies through the expedient of losing your minds is not the way to go. Consider what Paul says:

> The aged women likewise, that they be in behaviour as becometh holiness, not false accusers, not given to much wine, teachers of good things; That they may teach the young women to be sober, to love their husbands, to love their children, To be discreet, chaste, keepers at home, good, obedient to

their own husbands, that the word of God
be not blasphemed. (Titus 2:3–5)

I want to work through what is mentioned
here, but with a particular emphasis on what the
world is seeing as we seek to obey passages such
as this. So what does Paul teach here? The older
women in the church need to be holy in their
behavior (v. 3). They need to guard themselves
against speaking false accusations. In addition,
they should be careful to avoid a lot of wine; they
should be manifestly temperate in their behavior. While living this way, they should be teachers of good things—meaning that they should
be in a position to teach the younger women
how they should behave (v. 4).

They should instruct the younger women in
sobriety (v. 4) and the arts of domesticity (v. 4).
This is how I take the instruction on loving husbands and children. There are two words under-
neath that instruction, which are *philandros* and
philoteknos. The word for love here (*philo*) is a
word for warm affection, and in both instances it
is a compound word, together with the word for
man and the word for *children*. In a paraphrase, I
would render it as "teach them to be into husbands and into kids."

The older women are also to teach the younger women to be discrete and chaste, to be busy at home, good, obedient to their own husbands, so that the Word of God not be blasphemed. We are going to focus on that last phrase—*so that the Word of God not be blasphemed.*

So older wives are expressly taught to teach younger wives to subordinate themselves (*hypotasso*), so that the church does not get a bad reputation. The term is a military one, which does not make us think about following suggestions. Young men are commanded to be sober-minded also, doing good in all things, and again for the same reason—so that the one who is opposed has no evil thing to say about you. We are to live in a particular way—and in this instance it is young men being self-controlled—and we are to do it so that outsiders may not have anything evil to say about us. And slaves are commanded to be diligent and obedient also (*hypotasso* again). And why? So that they might adorn the doctrine of God (v. 10). The gospel is glorious, but Paul teaches that we, by our behavior, can adorn something that is already beautiful. That is what testimony is.

So which direction are we to lean? We are not just supposed to do what the Scripture says to do—although that is always important. We are also supposed to do it for the *reasons* that Scripture gives.

In other words, we must *let Scripture determine* how to head off what false ideas the pagans might have about us. Paul says here that the unbelievers should *see* the wife's submission and obedience. That is what is to be in the *foreground*. Paul does not say that submission and obedience must be in there somewhere, way in the background, but "make sure what they notice is how educated or witty you are."

No, Paul says that your unbelieving friends should notice what a sweetheart your husband has. At the risk of overstating it, let them find out how educated you are after they become Christians. I am not talking about hiding anything. I am talking about *not hiding* what God says to display.

So I am not saying that Christian women should hide their light under a bushel. I am saying that God tells us *what the light actually is*—the true light that shouldn't be under that bushel.

Being into the kids is the light that shouldn't be under the bushel.

This is because *God knows better than we do* what kind of thing will be attractive to unbelievers living in the midst of sexual and marital chaos. He knows what they need, and He knows what behavior on our part will churn them up inside. He knows all that, and He has told us all about it.

Allow me to illustrate the principle with another observation. The Christians who are most concerned with adjusting the "faith once delivered" to suit the sensitivities of unbelievers are the liberal Christians. And those who are the least concerned about it are the traditional dogmatic Christians. But as C.S. Lewis once pointed out, when atheists are converted it is almost never to the "broad-minded" forms of the faith. If they are going to be a Christian, they want to be an *actual* one. In the same way, an ardent feminist is unlikely to "convert" to the soft feminism of the evangelical edges.

And if unbelievers are not attracted to the order, harmony and hierarchy of Christian marriage, but rather remain in rebellion against it, this kind of testimony still stands as *potent*. If you are out at the park with your small tribe, and you get cold stares from angry lesbians, you are *not* bringing disrepute on the gospel. God says the opposite. God is in charge of what constitutes a good testimony in an age like ours. We have our marching orders.

Take this another way. Suppose God told Christian women to be modest (which, come to think of it, He did). Suppose further that all the women outside the church, or at least all the women who were *au courant*, were flappers. There are two ways to approach this. One says "I obviously need to be a flapper too, and so I need to figure out a way to sneak modesty in there somehow. And hope nobody notices." The other is to simply do what God instructs, and let the other pieces fall where they may.

GOSPEL AND MORE GOSPEL:

When we try to "gray out" the Christian forms of marriage that we practice, we are actually trying to "gray out" the gospel. Christ is the Bridegroom, and the Church is His Bride. Christian husbands are told to love their wives sacrificially, the way Christ loved His Bride (Eph. 5:25, 33). Christian wives are told to submit to their own husbands (Eph. 5:22, 33). Why would we try to hide this from the world? If they kick, let them kick. The dogs may bark at it, but the train keeps going. This is the good news of salvation, and we must not try to hide the fact that we have actual possession of it.

Husbands, your task is to model for the world what the objective gospel actually looks like. And, in case you have forgotten, it looks like blood, sweat, and tears. You are the hands of Christ as He preaches His message of salvation to the world, and never forget that those hands are pierced. You are *husbands*—you are to be pierced. You are the head. Does that tempt you to puff yourself up, as though that meant you were the King Boss? No, you are the *head*, and you are instructed to be the head the same way Jesus was. How was Jesus the head? Remember that if you are the head, you are supposed to have a crown of thorns jammed on it.

And wives, your task is to model for this lost world what a subjective and personal response to the gospel looks like.

As I have noted before, we are all limited, and we cannot *duplicate* what Christ did. But even though we cannot duplicate it, we are commanded to imitate it, and we are to imitate it as best we can.

Husbands, the world is watching you. You are to model what the *saving* looks like. Wives, the world is watching you. You are to model what the *salvation* looks like.

Why is the world not streaming to the rod of Jesse? Why are the nations not turning away from their folly? Is it because the gospel the Church is presenting to them is a gospel that looks too much like our marriages?

CHAPTER NINE

CHURCH AND KINGDOM, CATHEDRAL AND TOWN

R emember that the Spirit moves throughout the earth, converting and restoring individuals, fashioning them into saints, into believers. As His fruit is manifested in them, one of those fruits is self-control, self-government, or self-mastery. This self-government is the basic building block for establishing non-tyrannical governments in the other spheres that God has established among men. Without self-government, families can become autocratic tribes, with one domineering personality. Without self-government, the church can become a grasping and despotic monster, as happened with the medieval papacy. Without self-government, the civil magistrate can become an overweening and covetous thug, as has happened in our day.

It is easy for us to blame these governing entities for filling up the vacuum, but we really ought to find fault with ourselves because we (and our lack of self-control) are the ones who created the vacuum. When the people are slaves to sin, they *cannot* enjoy the balance of form and freedom that God has ordained for humanity. A family filled up with scheming manipulators will not be at peace with one another. A congregation of porn-users will not see the law of liberty unleashed in their midst. A nation of fornicating potheads will not enjoy civil liberty. You might as well expect to plant thistles and harvest barley.

> And the nations of them which are saved shall walk in the light of it: and the kings of the earth do bring their glory and honour into it. And the gates of it shall not be shut at all by day: for there shall be no night there. And they shall bring *the glory*

and honour of the nations into it. (Rev. 21:24-26, emphasis added)

In the midst of the street of it, and on either side of the river, was there the tree of life, which bare twelve manner of fruits, and yielded her fruit every month: and the leaves of the tree were for *the healing* of the *nations*. (Rev. 22:2, emphasis added)

Surely the isles shall wait for me, and the ships of Tarshish first, to bring thy sons from far, their silver and their gold with them, unto the name of the Lord thy God, and to the Holy One of Israel, because he hath glorified thee. And the sons of strangers shall build up thy walls, and their kings shall minister unto thee: for in my wrath I smote thee, but in my favour have I had mercy on thee. Therefore thy gates shall be open continually; they shall not be shut day nor night; that men may bring unto thee the forces of the Gentiles, *and that their kings may be brought.* (Isa. 60:9-11, emphasis added)

> And by the river upon the bank thereof, on this side and on that side, shall grow all trees for meat, whose leaf shall not fade, neither shall the fruit thereof be consumed: it shall bring forth new fruit according to his months, because *their waters they issued out of the sanctuary*: and the fruit thereof shall be for meat, and the leaf thereof for medicine. (Ezek. 47:12, emphasis added)

By mashing these texts together I am not attempting to pull a fast one, but am rather following the example of the New Testament writers, who frequently present us with a collage of quotations from all over the Old Testament.

In that spirit, the New Jerusalem in Revelation, the Isaianic Zion, and Ezekiel's great Temple, *are all one*. Comparing them with one another, and seeing what is said of them, we see that they are all symbolic images of the universal Christian Church, neither more nor less. The Jerusalem above is the mother of us all (Gal. 4:26). When we gather to worship God, we are assembled on the heavenly mountain, the heavenly Zion (Heb. 12:18). Come, the angel said to John, I will show you the Bride, the wife of the Lamb. And who is that Bride? It is the Christian Church

(Eph. 5:25). And then he showed him the New Jerusalem, adorned as a bride for her husband (Rev. 21:2). The great Harlot was the old Jerusalem, now divorced and put away. The New Jerusalem is the Holy of Holies, a living shrine of the living God (1 Cor. 3:16; 1 Cor. 6:19; Rev. 21:16). So much is basic.

My point with these texts is to show you the distinction between this Church and the redeemed nations of men. The boundary between them is porous, but is still clear. Ezekiel's Temple does not grow and fill the earth, but water flows *from* her until it inundates and heals the earth. The earth does not *become* the New Jerusalem, but the kings of the earth bring their honor and glory to her and acknowledge and support her. Kings will be nursing and nurturing fathers to the Church, and queens will be nursing mothers (Isa. 49:23). They simultaneously support the Church and submit to the Church. What they don't do is vaporize and float off. The great Zion of Isaiah does not swallow the world, but the ships of Tarshish sail to her, with all their wealth. There is an ongoing traffic of peace between them.

When men are forgiven and set upright again, they find themselves functioning within the framework of three basic governments. The first is the government of the family, following the order that God has established. The husband is the head, his wife is his body and the executive, and together they shepherd their little ones. The family is the ministry of health, education, and welfare. The second is the civil magistrate, which is the ministry of justice. Their task is to make it possible for you to walk across town safely at two in the morning. It is important to note that justice here is defined by the Bible, and not by the hurt feelings of somebody. The church is the ministry of grace and peace, who is the Holy Spirit Himself.

Every epistle in the New Testament begins with a reference to grace and peace, and this grace and peace is "from God the Father and our Lord Jesus Christ." The Holy Spirit is not mentioned directly, but I believe, following Jonathan Edwards, that this is because the Spirit *is* the grace and peace. The Church is therefore the place where the Holy Spirit is most in evidence, as He anoints the preaching, as He inhabits the praises of His people, and as He blesses the sacraments.

Because the word *justice* is so abused in our day, I need to say something brief about the civil magistrate's duty to enforce justice. Injustice is not the violation of autonomous human rights, however those rights may be defined. Injustice is the violation of God-given rights. God gave us all the right to a fair trial if we are accused of some crime. And so, if we get an unfair trial, the kind that Jesus got, this is an injustice. But God did not give us the "right" to fifteen dollars an hour. For if He did, that means that somebody else has the *obligation* to pay you that amount. And when the state steps in to enforce *that* kind of obligation, the result is always tyrannical.

So what is the relationship of these three governments?

In God's order, not one of the three is permitted to domineer over the others. Each has its assigned task, and each one needs to tend to its own knitting. The Church does not declare war, or collect the trash. The family does not administer the sacraments. The state does not review cases of church discipline. And not one of these spheres is dependent on any of the others for its existence.

Now in times of crisis, as when the city of Rome was threatened by the Lombards, one government may pick up some of the responsibilities of another. Say there is a failed state, but the Church is still present. Or in unusual circumstances, it may be a similar emergency, as when Paul prohibits Christians filing civil suits against one another before unbelieving judges (1 Cor. 6:1-7). Ordinarily, the church ought not to be adjudicating property line disputes, but we should prefer that to the scandal of asking pagans to define justice between two believers.

But with that said, there is definitely a hierarchy of honor in this glorious and eschatological fulfillment. And this is what it looks like. The Church does not fill up the world, and the Church does not make every day into Sunday. But the knowledge of the Lord *does* fill up the world, as the waters cover the sea (Hab. 2:14). How does this work?

In our texts, notice the flow in two directions. The living water flows *from* the Church out to all the families and nations of men, and all the families and nations of men flow to the Church.

But they don't stream to the Church in order to live there. They don't come into the Church to establish permanent residency. They come to eat from the tree of life, and then they go back out again into the world with a benediction upon them, with the peace of Christ upon their heads.

So picture it this way. The worship of God is central to all of life, but it does not devour all of life. The sun does not burn everything up, but it does give light to everything. The water does not flood the world, but it does irrigate the entire world. The anchor fastens the ship, the ship does not turn into a gigantic anchor. The cathedral is at the center of the town, but does not "take over" all the activities of the townspeople—their printing, their auto mechanics, their software designing, their lawn mowing. In one sense all of *that* is none of their business. But at the same time the church instructs the townspeople in the adverbs—*how* these things are to be done, meaning, honestly, before the Lord, with one eye always on the text, and with a hard work ethic.

The Church is therefore at the center of the kingdom, but the Church and the kingdom are still very different.

And Christ is Lord of all. So the authority of Jesus—the kind of authority that is granted to a sacrificial king—is an authority that mediates the kindness of the Father, and He mediates that kindness with the center fixed and all the edges in play. The Church teaches you how to be a father, but does not take over the role of a father. The Church instructs the magistrate, but does not rival the magistrate. The Church teaches wives to submit to their husbands, and models that submission through dutiful and cheerful submission to the authority of Christ as found in the Scriptures. Reflecting Christ, the Church suffuses all of life, the way sunlight fills up the day. It does not *displace* ordinary life, the way one billiard ball displaces another. Rather, it informs and instructs ordinary life—wherever you are in the town, out in the kingdom, whatever you are doing, whether changing a tire or changing a diaper, you can turn around and look, and from that place you can always see the church spire. And whenever you do, whatever you are doing, you are reminded that you are part of the Bride, the wife of the Lamb.

EPILOGUE

We are living in time when all the wheels appear to be coming off Pharaoh's chariots. But this should not distress us because we are Israelites, and we are already standing on the opposite shore.

We have forgotten that God frequently uses creative destruction in the advancement of His kingdom. Remember that the cross was His great victory, and it was cleverly disguised as a great disaster. So this should not distress us the way it frequently does. As G.K. Chesterton once put it in *The Everlasting Man*:

> Christendom has had a series of revolutions and in each one of them Christianity

has died. Christianity has died many times and risen again; for it had a God who knew the way out of the grave.[10]

We have a great opportunity before us. As Aslan once said to Lucy, when things were especially dark, "Courage, dear heart."

---

10. Christian Heritage Edition (Moscow, ID: Canon Press, 2020), 273.